Your Holistic Career Path

Create Career Change, Satisfaction, and Work/Life Balance

Lucy Appadoo

TABLE OF CONTENTS

MY TARGET AUDIENCE FOR THIS BOOK

This book is suitable for adults who are uncertain about their career. It is also appropriate for older, career-driven people who may be burnt out, looking for a new career, or wanting to shift their current career environment or culture within the same field. This book is for those who need guidance to find their true, meaningful career. It is not only about determining your true vocation but it's also about discovering what truly matters to you in all aspects of your life. Holistic living gives you meaning, joy, fulfilment, and purpose in life.

This book is also for those looking at a new career after an injury or mental illness and for those with a change of outlook, having grown out of a job after realising their current vocation no longer serves them. Outgrowing your career as you develop on a personal and spiritual level is common.

In this book, you will learn about career guidance, holistic well-being, stress management, diet, self-compassion and better work/life balance. You will also gain personal insight by identifying your values and long-term vision in life

INTRODUCTION

Do you feel your job no longer holds meaning for you? Maybe you've lost your sense of passion and fulfilment and feel like you're coming up empty. When was the last time you took a deep look at your career and lifestyle including work/life balance?

In this book, I will show you how to look at your life in a holistic way that can help you attain career fulfilment, overall well-being, and work/life balance.

Without insight and self-awareness, attaining a career that is appropriate for you will be more challenging. Do you need to make a positive change? Are you allowing obstacles to dictate your life? Why wait when positive change can be right on your doorstep? These days, you might switch your career multiple times, and along the way you may find that your current job no longer holds meaning for you. When was the last time you applied stress management strategies and practised work/life balance to give you the ability to see your life clearly?

As a registered counsellor, I have worked with clients who were no longer fulfilled in their jobs, were unable to find work/life balance, or were not sure about what steps to take to find a career that suited them. Other clients needed retraining after an injury or chronic medical condition. Still others were stressed and needed to reflect on how they could gain more satisfaction from their current career.

My work in vocational rehabilitation presented extensive challenges in multiple areas. For example, I had clients so horribly traumatised that no amount of therapy or medication would help to make them function well. Others had become too comfortable with unemployment and couldn't step out of their comfort zone. Some clients genuinely couldn't work because of a severe chronic or acute physical condition.

Attaining career satisfaction or making a career change involves constantly changing and growing on a personal level. For instance, you may have started out wanting to work with children. However, as you grew on a personal level and experiences shaped your beliefs, you developed a strong need to work with people struggling with grief. A career change may be necessary as you transition from an interest in working with children to a personal connection to grief counselling. For example, if you experienced the loss of multiple loved ones close together, a belief may form that makes you say to yourself, "I want to help people who have suffered as I have. I know what it's like to have cumulative grief." You therefore, might take the necessary training after developing self-awareness and an inner need and work as a grief counsellor.

Another example is when a mother loses her child to an accident caused by a drunk driver. She may then campaign to educate people about the dangers of drinking and driving. The experience has shaped her beliefs and eventually leads her to not only change her career but also redirect her purpose in life.

In terms of my own experience, I previously worked as an English as a second language teacher. After losing my baby son, I became a grief counsellor. I opened up to the support of my friends and family and spoke about how the loss affected me. I later reflected on my purpose and tried to make sense of his death. The loss led me to seek counselling. I wrote the biography of my son's ten-week life and created a memory box. These activities helped me to grieve, and I honour him with rituals (lighting candles, sharing his photos, visiting the cemetery) on special anniversaries. I was blessed to have known my son for ten weeks.

The experience of losing my son led me to a strong need to help others through the grieving process. Years later, I decided to specialise in grief counselling by studying and undertaking a twelve month internship as a grief counsellor one day per week. I currently enjoy working in grief and general counselling as part of my private counselling practice. I also work four days a week as a rehabilitation counsellor with the Australian government.

If you're not satisfied in your current job, you might take a different perspective to gain satisfaction if you're unable to leave the job. What can you do? You can look at the parts of the role that you do enjoy and strive to do more of those tasks. You can speak to your manager about a promotion if you feel that you've become stagnant and have additional skills to offer. You might decide to have a present-centred approach to your role by working slowly and taking in every detail mindfully. In other words, instead of taking action with your mind elsewhere, you could absorb yourself fully in the task without thinking about dinner for that night or what your plans are over the weekend. You will better appreciate your role and all it offers when you decide to get on with it, engaging fully with the task.

In terms of career satisfaction, you might decide to stay in a career that is unsatisfying but choose to have a side business or hobby that fulfils your creative passion and brings you joy. Other work or a hobby you enjoy in your spare time can make up for an unpleasant career. By partly fulfilling that passion outside of your regular work time, you could eventually develop a satisfying full-time career down the road.

PART ONE:

CAREER SELF-ASSESSMENT

Chapter One:

Identify Your Strengths

What are strengths? According to Martin Seligman in *Authentic Happiness* (2002), a strength is a trait or characteristic that is generally seen over a range of contexts over time. Strengths are also valued and create positive results. For instance, leadership ability can normally result in promotions, salary increases, and higher status. However, the strength can also be valued without any of those external rewards simply for the sheer enjoyment of it. Strengths can be considered values and skills learned over time, as well as innate aptitudes or talents.

I've helped clients in career counselling by asking them to identify their strengths. One approach is to take a test on strengths at www.authentichappiness.com to discover your top five strengths. You create a free account, log in, then choose "VIA Survey of Character Strengths" under the "Questionnaires" dropdown menu. You can also choose the "Brief Strengths Test" if you prefer. These tests are based on Martin Seligman's work on happiness and positive psychology. While it's optional, taking the strengths test will increase your understanding as you seek a new career direction.

Martin Seligman identified the following strengths under a range of different headings. Which strengths apply to you?

WISDOM AND KNOWLEDGE - the capacity to use your own knowledge and experience. Under this category are these strengths:

1. *Curiosity/Interest in the World*: You are open to experiences and are curious. You like to engage in novel experiences. You like to be challenged and are flexible with notions that don't exactly fit your worldview. The opposite of this would be you are easily bored.

2. *Love of Learning***:** You desire learning new things whether formally or independently. You previously enjoyed school, reading, and places that provided you with an opportunity to learn. You love learning for the sake of it and not for any other incentive behind it.

3. *Judgement/Critical Thinking/Open-Mindedness***:** You are able to make informed decisions as you rely on sound evidence to make those decisions. You also look at information from every angle to serve others well. Your thinking is practical and based in reality rather than on emotion (e.g., "it's usually my fault"). The opposite of this is thinking in ways that confirm irrational beliefs that you already have about yourself.

4. *Ingenuity/Originality/Practical Intelligence/Street Smarts***:** You desire something and are able to create practical steps to reach your goals. You are exceptionally creative in obtaining what you want, behaving in new ways or trying new approaches. You don't do things in a traditional manner.

5. *Social Intelligence/Personal Intelligence/Emotional Intelligence***:** This strength is knowing yourself and others. You're able to respond well to the emotions of others, and you notice changes in mood, temperament, motivations, and intentions; therefore, you're able to respond well on a social level. Personal intelligence is about knowing your own emotions and using that knowledge to facilitate your behaviour. This is also known as emotional intelligence.

6. *Perspective***:** Others require your guidance to solve problems as you have the wisdom or insight to see things from new perspectives. You are able to see the big picture.

COURAGE - The capacity to apply your will or intention even when there are challenges. You are brave, have perseverance, are honest, and have enthusiasm or zest.

7. *Valour and Bravery***:** You are willing to risk your life under great adversity. You also tend to have beliefs that are unpopular, difficult, or dangerous. You are able to face danger in spite of your fears.

8. *Perseverance/Industry/Diligence*: You complete challenging projects and have a strong work ethic. You don't complain about the work but complete it with flexibility and in a practical manner.

9. *Integrity/Genuineness/Honesty*: You're able to live a life that is true to you in an honest and genuine way. You're authentic, down-to-earth, and grounded. You do not have underlying motives but typically "tell it as it is" is to reveal your true self.

HUMANITY AND LOVE - The capacity to appreciate people around you by focusing and strengthening relationships. This means you have the ability to love and be loved, are kind or generous, and are socially and emotionally intelligent.

10. *Kindness and Generosity*: You're able to help others and are never too busy for them. You have empathy and sympathy towards others and assist them in spite of your own wishes, which take second place. You take responsibility for others and help them in times of need.

11. *Loving and Allowing Yourself to be Loved*: You enjoy close relationships and connections with others. Your friends and significant others value you, and you are able to accept their love.

JUSTICE - The capacity to be fair and responsible to yourself and others. This means you excel at teamwork, exhibit fairness, and have leadership qualities.

12. *Citizenship/Duty/Teamwork/Loyalty*: You work well as a team or group member. You pull your own weight for the benefit of group goals and respect authority. You sacrifice your own interests for the benefit of the group or team.

13. *Fairness and Equity*: You're able to make decisions based on fairness and rationale. You don't allow your personal feelings to bias your decisions. You give everyone a chance. You treat others equally no matter who they are, without prejudice or bias.

14.*Leadership*: You have the ability to plan activities for a group and ensure they are completed. You're able to relate to the group and resolve interpersonal conflicts.

TEMPERANCE - The capacity to be consistent and act with moderation. You are forgiving, merciful, modest, humble, wise, and self-regulating.

15.*Self-Control*: You're able to manage your emotions in challenging times. This means containing your desires, needs, and impulses when required so you can control your actions.

16. *Prudence/Discretion/Caution*: You have the ability to be careful and don't say or do things you may later regret. Longer-term success is more important to you than short-term goals or following sudden impulses. You ensure you have enough information at hand before taking action so you make the right choice.

17. *Humility and Modesty*: You don't boast about your achievements and don't view yourself as special or magical. You don't look for recognition or fame but prefer to let your achievements speak for themselves.

TRANSCENDENCE AND MEANING - The capacity to see a connection between the world around you and yourself. As a result, you have an appreciation of beauty, are grateful for things, have hope and humour, and are religious or spiritual.

18. *Appreciation of Beauty and Excellence*: You have an appreciation for aesthetics, brilliance, and skill in all areas, including nature, art, mathematics and science. You are inspired by these things and are elevated because of them.

19. *Gratitude*: You appreciate good things that happen to you. You appreciate nature and spirituality and like to take time to express your thanks. You take note when people do good in general and do good things for you. You notice everything as a blessing.

20. *Hope/Optimism/Future-Mindedness*: You like to plan for the future and have specific action plans in place. You are positive about the future. You believe you can have a great future if you work hard by setting specific goals.

21. *Spirituality/Sense of Purpose/Faith/Religiousness*: You believe in a higher purpose and meaning of the universe. Your beliefs apply to your actions and offer you security. You know where you fit in this life and what your calling or purpose in life entails. You find meaning in something larger than yourself.

22. *Forgiveness and Mercy*: You're able to forgive others who have done wrong by you. You prefer kindness and mercy rather than revenge. By forgiving others, you become more positive towards people who hurt you.

23. *Playfulness and Humour*: You enjoy laughing and making other people smile. You like to be playful rather than serious. You see the lighter side of life and like to be funny.

24. *Zest/Passion/Enthusiasm*: You tend to be excited about activities and look forward to your day. You're passionate about what you do and feel inspired by things. You are also very spirited and bounce with loads of energy.

As you can see, Martin Seligman identified many different strengths. He believed that most of these strengths will feel genuine to who you truly are, but one or two of them may not be who you are. For example, one of my previous client's top strengths included love of learning, fairness or justice, honesty or authenticity, diligence or perseverance, and spirituality or sense of purpose. Four of these felt authentic to his own true self, but fairness or justice wasn't a strength that he used often, if at all. It wasn't a preferred strength. For example, he does have a sense of justice and believes we're all equal; however, in times of great stress, he finds it difficult not to judge others, and his emotions can rule how he treats others. He tends to wear his heart on his sleeve under challenging times. It's a constant work in progress.

Another perspective on this is that one of these strengths may make you feel exhausted, but you still have the ability to apply that strength. You don't use it often, and it's not considered a signature strength.

Seligman states that your "signature strengths" are those you enjoy using in your daily life in work, love, and play. When looking at your top strengths, find out the following about each:

- Is this strength the real "you"?
- Are you excited by applying this strength, at least initially?
- Do you learn a lot by applying this strength?
- Do you want to learn new ways to apply this strength?
- Do you long to find ways to use this strength?
- Do you feel that you have to use this strength?
- Do you feel alive and energised after using this strength?
- Do you create tasks and personal projects around this strength?
- Do you experience joy, optimism, and energy while using this strength?

Seligman states that to attain career satisfaction, it's crucial to use your signature strengths daily on the job. Utilising strengths gives you joy, and transforms your job into a "calling," a job that is meaningful and holds value for you. Rather than having a job that is repetitive and routine, your work becomes gratifying and more important than the money you earn.

How else can you tell which personal strengths are most prominent in you? Here are some strategies:

- Take note of what others say you are efficient at. Notice compliments from others. You can confirm what others say about you by thinking of times when you practised those strengths.
- Make a list of your past successes and achievements. For example, writing a great report, winning a leadership award, or obtaining a promotion.

- Identify your hobbies and leisure time activities. Most likely, if you enjoy something you are also good at it. Examples may include cooking (creativity, generating ideas) or woodworking (good with your hands, creativity). Sometimes, your hobby can become a career or your own small business.
- Notice what you do day to day and how these activities make you feel. If you feel you've been productive and enjoyed an activity, most likely it's a strength. For example, organising and tidying a cluttered house in two hours demonstrates that you have the ability to create an organised environment amidst chaos.
- What is your current job description? Notice your efficiency in different aspects of the job to remind yourself of your skills and talents. For example, if your job involves teaching or mentoring others, then your strengths are leadership and teaching.

After discovering your personal/signature strengths, use them often and in many situations. You can use these strengths daily in work or career, social contexts, parenting, and leisure.

Chapter Two:

Recognise Your Values

Values are similar to strengths. Russ Harris, in *ACT Made Simple* (2009), defines values as your heart's deepest desires in relation to how you want to interact with society, other people, and yourself. Values are about how you want to behave, the kind of person you want to be, and the kinds of strengths and qualities you want to develop. For example, if you choose to play tennis, what qualities or strengths do you utilise? How do you want to behave in your interactions with other tennis players on your team and your opponents? The answers to these questions might be to be focused, competitive, fair, willing to extend yourself, respectful, and cooperative with other players. The qualities you choose to show through your actions are dictated by your values; by what's important to you, not by a sense of obligation or what you feel you should do.

Another example is a woman who desires to care for and raise children because she is nurturing and helpful. However, she is unable to do that if she cannot conceive. There goes her dream—or does it? What if she chose other avenues of fulfilling her value of being nurturing and helpful with children? She could choose to work in childcare or she could undertake volunteer work in this industry. She could also devote significant time and energy to the children of her family members. All it takes is a resourceful move to have those needs met when you feel the odds are against you.

Research has shown that as we age, we turn more towards meaning and fulfilment rather than money and material success. How do you want to be?

The difference between values and goals is this: Values are desired qualities of ongoing action, such as being helpful, caring, focused, and nurturing. Goals are things you want to achieve or complete.

An example in relation to a career would be having a goal of getting promoted to manager (goal); values in this case could be leadership, diligence, and courage. The same distinction between goals and values applies to the example of the woman who has the values of being nurturing and helpful and wants to achieve the goal of having children.

What are your values and goals in relation to your current or future career? Are you living by your values at the moment? If not, what do you need to do to fulfil your deepest values so you can achieve your goals?

Personal values include your work needs in terms of what's important for you to express through your career and how your values can be productive to the community. When your values are aligned with your career, you tend to be quite satisfied. If they are not, you'll be thinking about changing careers rather quickly. Your values are an important part of making decisions about your current career or a change of career; they are what make you feel of value as you contribute to society in a productive way. Values could include connecting with others, creative expression, having the authority to make important decisions, feeling secure in your career, having an influence over others, and so on.

My values include helping others, nurturing my daughters and family, and engaging in spiritual pursuits. I fulfil these values by working as a counsellor, raising my two daughters with love and mindfulness, and practicing meditation, prayer, and meaningful activity.

Using Shadow Cards and Strength Cards to Build Self-Awareness of Values

Shadow cards are tools that invite you to explore the parts of yourself that are difficult to talk or think about. Each card shows a glimpse into the hidden parts of yourself that you avoid or that only show up at a subconscious (unknown) level. The cards might show fears, sadness, challenges, distress, and also the positive parts of yourself that you might struggle to accept. They can provide insight for positive change.

You can use the shadow cards in the resource section for grief and loss, to inspire creative writing, and as a conversational tool. It's good to remember that when you're under stress, you need to take a step back so you can begin to apply your values to your career or life.

The pictures of the shadows were inspired by mysticism and Carl Jung (physician and psychiatrist). Only the person who selects the cards can interpret what the pictures mean. When I use shadow cards, I ask clients what their interpretation of the card is and how it resonates with them.

For example, one of my clients selected a card that showed a jogger hunched over and exhausted outside a house. The client interpreted this card to mean that she was physically and emotionally exhausted and was no longer able to run that marathon. She was burnt-out at home and needed respite. In actuality, her husband had died and she was struggling to raise her two children alone. The card enabled her to cry for help, and we discussed how she could get that respite and the kind of support she needed so her health could become a priority.

Another interpretation of the jogger shadow card might be that you need timeout from your work or you may need to slow down due to burn-out. The cards enable you to tap into what your subconscious knows you need on a deeper level. Every card has its own meaning and interpretation, depending on what is going on in your life at that moment. Your subconscious mind will draw you to a particular card or cards infused with meaning and depth. The cards are selected face-up, but the idea is to choose the cards you feel connected to.

Another set of tools for self-awareness are strength cards. Strength cards are great for insight into your positive qualities, values, career journey, and how experiences affect who you are on par with your values, skills, and material resources. You can draw on these strengths to manage challenges in everyday life.

Strength cards demonstrate your freedom to choose. You can choose to be resilient, calm, or curious in spite of the things in life you cannot control. These are resources you can draw from when you're feeling down and empty and when you lose sight of who you are and what your capacities are.

The strength cards give you a voice and acknowledge what you already know. On a subconscious level, you know what you need, and these cards can help you pick up on that energy at a deeper level.

For example, my client who had lost her husband and was raising two children alone selected cards that stated "I can choose to be resilient" and "I can choose to be calm." With the first card, we brainstormed ways she could be resilient. We decided she could compartmentalise her grief when she needed to care for her children and make them feel secure. I encouraged her to express her grief and help her children understand that grief is normal but suggested she could also demonstrate her resilience by picking herself up and moving on with things. She could put her grief into a box and bring it out later to make sense of it.

With the second card, my client decided to take time away from home by asking her sister out for a coffee while their mother cared for her children. She realised she needed respite and time away to spend quality time without the children.

Chapter Three:

Practise Self-Compassion

Self- compassion is noticing when you are suffering and having sympathy towards yourself. In other words, you are warm and understanding towards yourself whenever you are suffering, fail at something, or notice a flaw. Rather than judging or criticising yourself for your weaknesses, you are kind and nurturing towards yourself. You realise that you are human and therefore not perfect (Neff, 2015).

When you live according to your values and set goals, you need to exercise self-compassion. If you don't, you'll struggle to achieve your goals and live by your values. In other words, when you judge yourself harshly based on your weaknesses and flaws, you feel badly about yourself, lose confidence, and have poor motivation to act. As a result, your ability to take action based on your values and strengths is impacted. In fact, you most likely will not have clearly identified your values and strengths when you feel badly about yourself and your life.

Self-compassion involves having a balanced take on your negative emotions. Your emotions aren't ignored but are acknowledged and validated. When you're self-compassionate, you notice your emotions without judging them so you don't become enmeshed in the emotions. You also realise that emotions or thoughts are part of the human experience. You say to yourself, "I am noticing that I feel angry right now" or "I am aware that I am feeling sad about this situation," and that's okay. You gain some distance from your emotions this way and come to accept them.

How You Can Use Mindfulness with Self-Compassion

Russ Harris described mindfulness as paying attention with flexibility, openness, and curiosity. In other words, mindfulness is a process of awareness by which you notice your experience in the present moment and accepting it in spite of not liking the experience. Rather than resisting a negative thought or experience, you acknowledge and notice it without judgement. This can help you live your life according to your values in spite of your fears or weaknesses. For example, if you're scared to apply for a leadership promotion at work as you believe you'll fail, that fear does not stop you from applying. You validate your thought but continue to act in spite of it. You don't let your thoughts or emotions rule your life; instead, you take action.

Another example is when you're not coping with new responsibilities at work because you lack the proper training. Rather than beat yourself up about it, you acknowledge the thought. You can then decide to seek training or speak to your manager about returning to your original job. Particularly with weaknesses, you must decide to let something go or secure new skills.

Mindfulness and self-compassion are connected as both involve a state of being present and accepting yourself as you are. They are also about accepting situations that can't be changed. You don't judge and have self-awareness. Mindfulness originated from the early teachings of the Buddha. For further information, visit http://www.actmindfully.com.au/.

An Exercise to Demonstrate How You Can Use Self-Compassion

An exercise to build mindful awareness is to use clear or coloured glass stones or large marbles for sensory awareness. The purpose is to keep yourself grounded whenever you're under stress, allowing you to remain in the present. The steps for this exercise are:

- Handle the stone or marble in the palm of your hand and feel the texture. Is it smooth, rough, cold, hot, warm?
- What does the stone or marble look like? Are there any patterns, colours, light, or shade?
- What is the shape? Is it oblong, round, distorted?

- Close your eyes and think about whether the stone elicits any positive memories. Does it remind you of a childhood holiday or the times you travelled to the beach during the summer?

The sensory detail of the exercise takes you to a place of greater awareness and perspective. You appreciate the textures of the stones or marbles, and that offers a distraction from stress. The exercise can associate your distress with something positive and grounding (hence the smooth textures of the stones or marbles).

If you feel stressed about your current career or stuck on career change, the exercise allows you to get in touch with bodily feelings, which grounds you in the moment so you establish self-awareness. Self-awareness leads to insight into your values in reference to your passion or dream career.

How Does Self-Compassion Relate to Career Guidance?

Having an accurate assessment of your strengths, values, and weaknesses will be reflected in the type of career you seek. If you're accepting of particular weaknesses and notice them with mindful attention, you may decide to work on those weaknesses if they're relevant to your life and career. You will also have an understanding and acceptance of your strengths, which will reflect in your chosen career.

For example, if you choose to apply for a management position but your weakness is conflict-resolution, you may decide to do training in this area or be mentored/coached on this particular topic. If the position is important for your overall well-being, you'll find a way to reach your goal. On the other hand, if you become too caught up in or upset about your weaknesses, thinking, "I'm so stupid," rather than having a mindful awareness of the weakness, you will fall into the trap of berating yourself. This will not motivate you to work on that weakness but will cause you to wallow in misery.

You need to remind yourself that you're human and that your self-development is your choice. You *can choose* to wallow in misery and be self-critical or you can be accepting and aware of your weakness and let that propel you into taking action to correct the weakness. You may also decide not to do anything at all, particularly if you have no desire to apply for a leadership role. However, particular strengths and skills can be useful not only in the vocational field, but also for general well-being.

Case Study to Demonstrate How You Can Use Self-Compassion

The following is an exercise I used with a private client who felt inadequate in his new role as a youth worker. In this exercise, he dealt with his inner critic. The exercise originated from Gestalt Therapy (visit www.gestalttherapyaustralia.com.au for further information) and involves working with three empty chairs arranged in a triangle.

I started by explaining the process whereby my client would be speaking to different aspects of himself represented by the chairs. One chair was the voice of the inner critic, another chair was the voice of the part of him that feels judged and criticised, and another chair was the voice of a wise, compassionate observer.

I had my client contemplate the inadequacy he felt at work and then sit in the chair representing his inner critic. As he sat in that chair, he expressed loudly what this aspect of himself was thinking and feeling. For instance, "I don't like the way you can't speak up for yourself. You're so weak."

I then asked the client to sit in the chair representing the part of him that feels judged and criticised, telling him to get in touch with how he feels about his inner critic. Then I asked him to express how he felt. He said, "I feel extremely hurt. You don't help me at all."

I then asked him to have a conversation between these two aspects of himself, moving from one chair to the other. I told him to get fully in touch with each aspect so he knew how each of them felt. Each aspect must fully express its opinions.

I finally instructed the client to take the chair representing the compassionate observer. Here, the client needed to get in touch with his deepest intuition and understanding to address both the inner critic and the aspect of self that is judged. I asked, "What does your compassionate self have to say to the other aspects?" He replied, "You have taken on the voice of your father." Or "I can see how scared you are and how you're trying to keep me on guard so I don't make mistakes. You just want to be accepted for who you are."

At the end of the exercise, we discussed the session. My client said he found it to be a great tension releaser, having gained new insights and perspectives. He now understood these different voices and would most likely become more detached when the inner critic presented itself. For example, he might say, "I take note of your criticism and I will learn from this," rather than become all flustered and emotional. The exercise is a self-compassionate way of being mindful of your surroundings.

Another client created a self-compassion journal. This involves writing in the evening to review the events of the day. You can write about anything that went wrong— your self-judgements, your challenges—and try to make sense of your day. Be kind to yourself, knowing that you are human and bound to make mistakes. Learn from them, and endeavour to not repeat them. For example, you can evaluate your judgements by saying you made a mistake at work because you had other things on your mind or perhaps you didn't have enough sleep. Subsequently, you learn to find ways to stay focused and ensure you get enough sleep.

Personally, if I make mistakes, I reflect and take note of how to improve on something. If I realise that a particular task is not my strength, I rely on help from others and accept that I've tried. I live with no regrets as I try to do things for myself first, particularly in the area of technology (I require assistance with this). I recite the following affirmation: *May I be safe; may I be peaceful, may I be kind to myself, and may I accept myself as I am.*

Use self-compassion to nurture yourself and your career. The exercises and examples show the effectiveness of doing so.

Chapter Four:

John Holland's Personality Types and Environment

Your personality determines what kinds of conditions or work environment you'd like and the type of career you choose.

Psychologist John Holland developed a theory of career and vocational choice based on people's personality types. These include the Doers (Realistic), the Thinkers (Investigative), the Creators (Artistic), the Helpers (Social), the Persuaders (Enterprising), and the Organisers (Conventional).

Doers (Realistic) are practical, stable, persistent, and down-to-earth types. These people prefer "things" rather than ideas or people. They enjoy being outdoors, using tools or machinery, working with their hands, and working with animals. They are concrete thinkers. A sample of jobs from this personality type include musician, fashion designer, chef, fire-fighter, carpenter, agricultural worker, veterinarian, and driver.

Thinkers (Investigative) are introspective and like to use their mind to analyse things. They have an inquiring, rational mind so prefer to explore and investigate. Jobs associated with this personality type include a lawyer, nurse, professor, zoologist, dentist, computer engineer, surgeon, psychologist, dietician, and pharmacist.

Creators (Artistic) are creative, intuitive, sensitive, and expressive. These people rely on their feelings and imagination, and have inspirational and innovative ideas. Jobs suited to this personality type include fashion designer, fine artist, interior decorator, public relations professional, photographer, web designer, graphic designer, chef, and musician.

Helpers (Social) are kind, patient, cooperative, empathetic, tactful, friendly, and helpful. These people enjoy activities comprising social activity, helping others, teaching, teamwork, and building relationships. They are guided towards offering a service and have good interpersonal skills. Jobs suited to this personality type include clergyperson, counsellor, community organiser, dietician, fitness trainer, lawyer, social worker, psychologist, surgeon, trainer, veterinarian, teacher, and physician.

Persuaders (Enterprising) are ambitious, outgoing, energetic, confident, and enjoy challenges. They enjoy work that comprises leadership, business, public speaking, risk-taking, and politics. Types of jobs suited to this personality type include architect, fire-fighter, broadcast journalist, market research analyst, real estate agent, lawyer, business executive, management consultant, fundraiser, and educational administrator.

Organisers (Conventional) are analytical, efficient, accurate, organised, and conservative. They enjoy activities involving structure and practical tasks and like to have rules to follow. They thrive in office settings doing such work as accounting, statistics, numeracy, and mathematics. Jobs suited to this personality type include technical writer, computer engineer, maths teacher, pharmacist, business trainer, archivist/librarian, educational administrator, nurse, and financial officer.

Cross-Matching Careers With Personality Types

As you can see from the range of personality types, a variety of careers mesh with a combination of personality types, so matching your career to your personality is not completely black and white. A single career or role can match to different personality types and may depend on the kind of environment, conditions and type of industry in which the role is performed. For example, a nurse can be a conventional type who requires good attention to detail and accuracy. However, a nurse also requires strong helping or interpersonal skills, given the work involves communication, empathy, and assistance/service.

Personal Qualities and Careers

Your personal qualities or traits are generally innate and part of who you are rather than learned, as skills tend to be. Personal qualities arise in various contexts and may be good within some contexts and not so good at other times. For example, aggression is useful for a sports-related person, but not so effective for a counsellor. Examples of personal qualities or traits include ambition, assertiveness, calmness, tactfulness, curiosity, friendliness, honesty, enthusiasm, independence, motivation, patience, precision, punctuality, resourcefulness, shyness, practicality, loyalty, responsibility, sensitivity, and so on. What are your personal qualities, and how are they useful or not useful in your current or prospective career?

Extroverts and Introverts

Extroverts or outgoing people are most likely to prefer changes and lots of action. They enjoy getting to know new people and like face-to-face contact. They tend to want things to happen quickly so will enjoy a fast-paced work culture. They also like to be part of a team and do not favour working alone. They may be impulsive and may make rash decisions.

Introverts, on the other hand, derive energy from quiet environments. They're happy to work alone. They also make cautious decisions, preferring to have all the information at hand before making a decision. They also like to focus on a task without being interrupted. They tend to be quiet achievers and like to learn by reading or searching the internet.

Are you an introvert or an extrovert? Are you aware of the kinds of working conditions you like and dislike?

Chapter Five:

Self-Assessment of Skills, Aptitudes, Interests, and Desired Level of Responsibility

Listing your skills, aptitudes, interests, and desired level of responsibility can help you determine what kind of career is right for you. The information below can help you do this. It is summarised from an Australian Government workbook entitled *Finding the Right Direction - Career Planning Workbook* (2006).

Skills can be categorised as either general skills or work-related skills. General skills can be learned through higher level courses, schooling, home life, work, and from other people. For example, you might have learned to mentor and help others, so you have leadership or teaching skills. You might have organised your child's birthday party using your research skills by looking at a range of places to hold the party. You then might have called these venues to discuss availability using your communication skills. Finally, when discussing the price, you might have used your negotiation skills. What general skills do you have?

Work-related skills are tasks you're able to do for a particular job. You might be able to use a spreadsheet or have computer skills for a bookkeeping job, be able to provide great customer service for a retail position, or be able to draw blood for a nursing position. Think about the current work-related skills you possess and whether they're transferable to other jobs. For example, customer service skills are useful for both retail and hospitality roles. Counselling skills are useful for work as a counsellor or teacher. What are your transferable work-related skills?

Aptitudes are tasks you're naturally good at. These are innate gifts. People you know might say you have a natural ability for design or creativity. You might also have good coordination or be naturally well-organised. You might have a gift or aptitude for cooking or crafts. What are your aptitudes?

Interests are hobbies and things you like to do in your spare time. Your interests may include being involved in clubs, community groups, church groups, hobbies, or arts and crafts. Could these things you're involved in become a paid career?

The level of responsibility you desire in your career depends on your general lifestyle and your experience on the job. You might prefer work/life balance, so you'd rather not have the responsibility of being a supervisor high up the ladder managing a large team. You may be starting out in your career and willing to have a lot of responsibilities as you gain more experience. You might be ambitious, so you want a responsible position that allows you to move up the hierarchy with a higher salary. Are you happy with the level of responsibility you have in your career at the moment, or would you like training or experience that leads to a greater level of responsibility? Does the level of responsibility you crave mean you'll need to look at a different type of career or the same career with a different organisation?

According to *The Home Therapist* by Dr John Barletta and Jan Bond (2012), you need self-awareness when making career choices or changing your current career. You need to ask yourself where you fit in and what type of work suits you. You also require awareness of the world of work in order to determine the types of career choices you have.

To gain self-awareness, ask yourself about the type of environment in which you'd like to work. For example, do you prefer working indoors or outdoors, in a sedentary role or a physical role? Do you like predictable tasks or ones involving variety?

Ask yourself about the type of work that interests you. For instance, do you prefer helping others and/or the community? Do you like managing others and mentoring? Do you favour hands-on activities? Do you like to find solutions and determine outcomes with innovative ideas?

In terms of your talents, aptitudes and skills, what are your strengths? Do you like practical tasks? Do you prefer speaking to others? How do you feel about working with numbers and facts? Are you more on the creative and expressive side? Do you like to come up with solutions to problems?

Ask yourself about the kind of environment that suits your personality. Are you energised by communicating with a lot of people, or do you prefer a quiet environment? Do you like facts and numbers rather than dilemmas? Do you like rules and structure, or do you prefer having flexibility? Do you prefer logical answers or decisions based on how people feel?

Generally, having an understanding of skills, aptitudes, interests, desired level of responsibility, and self-reflection/awareness is crucial to determining which work environment is best suited to your career needs and personality style.

Specific Skill Sets

It's crucial to ask yourself the following questions about your everyday activities. The list is not exhaustive but gives you an idea on how to reflect on what you do daily. Reflecting on these daily tasks can give you a glimpse into how the skills or personal qualities involved match with your career choices. It can deepen your awareness of transferable skills that will make you a winner in an employer's eyes. The questions and comments are summarised from *I Can Do that Too- How to Count Your Work Skills* (Commonwealth of Australia, 1998).

- **Getting Around** - Do you have a sense of direction or can you follow a map? If so, you have planning and information-gathering skills. Can you plan a holiday and find the cheapest option available? If so, you have research and forward-thinking skills.
- **Managing Households** - Can you organise your budget and commit to it? Can you complete your tax return? If so, you have financial, budgeting, and planning skills.

- **Clothes** - Are you able to mix and match your limited clothing most of the time? Can you sew your own clothes? If so, you are resourceful, stylish, have design skills, and have good attention to detail.
- **Food -** Have you ever organised a dinner party with someone else? If you don't have certain ingredients, can you use similar ingredients? If so, you have team-building skills and are able to delegate, as well as have flexibility, creativity, and lateral-thinking skills.
- **Around the Home -** Do you like fixing things? Are you able to find things in your home when they're not in their usual place? If so, you have problem-solving skills and are able to use tools. You also have patience.
- **Friends and Family** - Can you cope with crises? Do you organise family events? If so, you have leadership skills, project management skills, and organisational ability.
- **In the Community** - Have you had your own stall at a market or fete? Are you good at writing letters, reports, pamphlets, or newsletters? If so, you have marketing and co-ordination skills, literacy, editing, and design skills.
- **Interests and Hobbies** - Are you able to create a video from your ideas? Do you collect stamps or coins and look for missing items to complete your collection? If so, you have technical and artistic skills. You also have cataloguing skills, attention to detail, and specialist knowledge.
- **Children and Young People -** Do you like caring for children, and do they enjoy being with you? Have you ever helped someone manage their difficult teenage child? If so, you have child-rearing skills, patience, imagination, and responsibility. You also have counselling skills, are nurturing, can mentor, and have empathy.
- **Social and Personal** - Have you ever had a garage sale or sold things you made at a market? Do you welcome new people into your area and tell them how things work in the community? If so, you have business and marketing skills. You also have public relations skills, interpersonal skills, and are able to share information.

Chapter Six:

Take Career Planning Action

This chapter outlines how to plan your career, taking your overall strengths, values, personality style, work environment, and skills into consideration.

According to *Handbook on Career Counselling—A Practical Manual for Developing, Implementing and Assessing Career Counselling Services in Higher Educational Settings* (United Nations Educational, Scientific and Cultural Organisation, 2002), you need to have an understanding of where you belong in the world and the type of roles you're suited to (self-awareness). You also need to know what jobs are out there and what the jobs are like (world-of-work awareness). In other words, when planning a career, you need to establish self-awareness in terms of your interests, values, skills, and personal preferences. You also need to connect self-awareness to career exploration. You can use an online job guide, or complete a career quiz or inventory (e.g. http://joboutlook.gov.au).

When researching a career, look for the following:
- Training required
- Job description or role
- Related careers or jobs
- Career Growth/Prospects of the role and salary
- Links to other resources, including websites, training institutions, and professional associations

Once you've researched the kind of career you're interested in, you can take the following career-planning action or steps:
- Update your resume and target it to the types of jobs you're applying for.

- Research industries and employers in the areas you'd like to work. You might search on the internet, peruse job advertisements in the newspaper, link in with a recruitment agency, talk to friends and family, or visit university career centres and talk to career counsellors. You can also attend career exhibitions or job expos, trade shows, and college open days and speak to others already working in the industry.
- Network with employers to discover the hidden job market. This means you might cold-canvas by ringing or meeting potential employers to enquire about positions that are not advertised. You might follow up on a lead to speak to an employer about on open position recommended by someone else (warm-canvassing).
- Use social media to establish professional networks on sites such as LinkedIn, Facebook, or Twitter. Ensure you have a professional profile so you can portray yourself in a business-like fashion. Take care of what you post on these sites, and use appropriate language.
- Apply for positions by writing a customised letter and having a targeted resume. For the hidden job market, you might have already provided a resume without a letter unless the employer specifically asked for a formal application.
- Prepare for interviews by researching the employer or company. Do a mock interview and have some anticipated questions prepared. Many interviews are behaviour-based; for example, you might be asked about a time when you had a strict deadline to meet. You might also be asked standard questions, such as what are your strengths?
- Get to the interview earlier than the scheduled time so you don't rush, and dress appropriately.

Take the time to map out a structured set of steps, and treat your job-search like a job itself. If you're looking for a full-time position, you need to take a full-time approach to job seeking. Then in no time, your career planning action will lead to reaching your goal.

Chapter Seven:

Learn through Case Studies - Vocational Rehabilitation

While working for seven years in vocational rehabilitation, I performed assessments for Work Cover clients participating in a two-year program. They had experienced a physical injury, developed a chronic illness, or presented with mental health conditions and could no longer perform the work they had previously done. They were either too ill to return to work, had become fearful of returning to work, or did not know what other kinds of work they could perform.

Grief and loss became a part of their lives as they struggled to adjust to a life with limitations. Identity crises occurred; they questioned who they were and where their lives were going. These clients' lives were filled with pain and physical limitations that restricted their ability to perform daily household tasks, shop, catch public transport, drive, and use previously established skills.

This group disliked their restricted life yet resisted embracing a new one. Their confidence was low, they rejected options for retraining, and they were afraid to return to work. What work could they do anyway? Which employer would hire them in any case? They felt useless, like rubbish, so why not fall into the scrap heap? Why not give up, as that was the surest way for their identity to remain intact?

I worked with people of all ages, backgrounds, and conditions. While a few were motivated, many were not. However, there were good news stories.

For example, I worked with a 23-year old male who had difficulty managing anger, former substance abuse issues (he was at risk for relapse), and a back condition. He attended appointments fortnightly with a negative mindset and believed wholeheartedly that, given his multiple issues, an employer would never hire him.

I asked him questions to motivate him while acknowledging his resistance, and together we created goals. In order to shift his mindset, he needed a voice to acknowledge and validate his thoughts and emotions. He'd had a limited work history in the hospitality sector, so I organised a work experience program in a takeaway shop. He worked there for almost two weeks, and enjoyed it. While he was happy with the support he received from the staff, he was even more elated when the manager offered him some casual work once he completed his work experience program. He was ecstatic, and his self-confidence skyrocketed.

Feeling like he was on track, he finally started to believe in himself. However, once he'd completed his work experience program, the owner withdrew her offer, stating they wouldn't be able to offer my client work due to their budget. This client drew back into his shell. All the work we had done unravelled, and we were back to square one. He was angry, hurt, sad, and annoyed. For a while, he refused to look at other options. I gave him space to vent so he could process the loss of the job and eventually learn from the experience. I also organised woodwork training for him as he had an interest in making things with his hands. However, this fell through as he decided to look for paid work instead.

I worked with a specialised employment consultant to look at other job options. This client was good with his hands, so the employment consultant found him a job building cubby houses. We applied for the position on his behalf, he attended an interview, and he was later offered a full-time position. We monitored him for six months. Towards the end of our vocational program, we found out he had moved on to a manager's position. He was loving the job and had found his calling. After finishing the program, he became an independent worker.

This example demonstrates how a negative mindset influences emotion and behaviour, leading to either inaction or the wrong action. It also demonstrates how motivating oneself to look at other options, being resourceful, and drawing on social support is effective for those with physical or mental health issues. You can never give up, as each negative experience tests your strength and inner resources.

A Longer Case Study

As a rehabilitation consultant/case manager, I worked with insurers and Work Cover to assess clients going through the Work cover process as a result of a workplace injury or accident. I completed vocational assessment reports for the purpose of either returning these people to the same position (with lighter duties) or recommending other positions that would not aggravate their injury and would allow them time to recover.

One such case I handled was a 37-year old male referred by his insurer for a vocational assessment. To maintain confidentiality, I will present the case in general with an altered name.

John sustained a herniated disc whilst lifting a heavy object in the workplace. This resulted in a diagnosis of lumbar disc pain. He was treated with pain medication, received physiotherapy, attended a pain management clinic, and underwent acupuncture. Surgery was an option if his condition didn't improve. He was also diagnosed with depression due to his chronic pain. In addition to taking antidepressants, he attended counselling sessions with a psychologist.

John's barriers to a new career, after an absence from the workplace for seven years, included not being able to sit for more than forty minutes, an inability to stand for more than thirty minutes, limited ability to bend, difficulty undertaking various household tasks such as washing dishes and vacuuming, an inability to lift more than ten kilograms, and an inability to drive due to ongoing pain. It was obvious from the impact of John's condition that he was unable to return to his previous position, which required heavy lifting.

I administered a test used to determine the types of thoughts and feelings people have when they experience pain. John had strong thoughts about his pain and a sense of helplessness. His scores were not clinically significant, but the issues impacted his return to work program with Work Cover.

I also performed a test that evaluates confidence levels for people with chronic pain while performing activities when in pain. John demonstrated a clinically significant score of 24. Any score under 30 shows a low level of confidence about returning to work, so John's score was quite low.

I asked John about coping strategies, and he stated that during times of distress he distracted himself with television, drawing, reading, and photo restoration. In previous sessions, he had mentioned he enjoyed restoring family photographs.

I also asked John about vocational training to investigate alternative career options, and he stated that he had an interest in a career in early childhood education once his pain levels improved.

Transferable skills based on John's previous work history included the following:
- Customer service and cash-handling skills
- Strong written and verbal skills
- Italian language speaking skills
- Sound computer skills
- Reception skills (responding to telephone queries, faxing, photocopying, taking messages)
- Basic filing
- Retail sales experience
- Experience restoring old photographs

Personal attributes John identified included:
- Creative
- Friendly
- Quick learner
- Proactive
- Well-organised
- Ability to multitask
- Good social interactions

- Enjoyment of learning

Work interests/preferences and values John expressed included:
- Call centre work
- Photo restorations or photographer's assistant
- Child care or preschool teaching in the longer term
- Home-based computer work (web design, graphics); however, this type of work would require further training.

I did a labour market analysis via the labour market site Archangel and the Australian Job Search website in 2008 for work as a photographer's assistant doing photo restorations. The results showed that most of these positions were full-time. Sixty-eight percent of jobs were in photographic studios and shopfronts, 13 percent in business services, 7 percent in the photographic processing industry, and 5 percent in cultural services, especially museums. No photo restoration jobs were advertised on Seek or the Australian Job Search website in 2008, but Google displayed 29,100 results for photo restoration work.

I then did a labour market analysis via Archangel and Australian Job Search for work as a call centre operator.

The results showed that most call centre operator jobs in Australia were part-time. Thirty-three percent of jobs were in business services, 12 percent in retail, 10 percent in health and community services, 8 percent in manufacturing, 8 percent in finance and insurance, 7 percent in wholesales, and 6 percent in communication services. Seek displayed 35 jobs in the call centre industry, while the Australian Job Search website displayed 11 jobs in the northern region.

Overall, taking into account John's interests, skills, experience, and physical restrictions along with labour market analyses, John narrowed the vocational options down to photo restorations and call centre work with modifications (an adjustable chair and frequent breaks for changes of posture). John felt he'd be able to do these jobs because of his experience in photo restoration and customer service skills, as well as his ability to converse with a wide range of people.

I recommended that John have ongoing psychological counselling to assist him with his beliefs about his pain and improve his self-confidence. I also suggested that an occupational therapist could help him assess the work environment to improve his performance. He would also require assistance with job seeking, as he had been out of the workforce for seven years, so I suggested that a job search group or individual case management would be useful, as well as a possible referral to a pain management clinic that could guide John to manage his pain and learn relaxation methods to reduce symptoms.

Overall, John had a number of vocational options to pursue and strategies to address his personal barriers. He had learned to manage his pain and started volunteer work with a photographer with the hope that he would eventually attain paid work in this field.

PART TWO:

SELF CARE

Chapter Eight:

Manage Your Stress

Being unhappy with your career is stressful, as is job hunting and starting a new job. While you go through these experiences, it's helpful to learn how to manage stress so your chance of finding work increases. Under stress, you're less likely to find work, as you're not feeling well physically, mentally, or spiritually. This chapter identifies a range of stress management strategies that provide holistic health and well-being.

According to the Mental Health Foundation, stress involves tension or pressure that is overwhelming and difficult to manage. Ultimately, it can have physical or emotional consequences or symptoms. Stress has many causes, including major life events, such as marriage, divorce, unemployment, moving house, and grief and loss. Minor stressors may include feeling unappreciated by your spouse, managing rebellious children, or burnout at work.

Stress is positive when it improves your performance. It can keep you on your toes and give you ideas to help you work harder and challenge yourself. Some people work better under stress as they find it energising and exciting. However, ongoing stress can result in sickness and fatigue. If it's not addressed, stress can even kill you.

While stressed, your body creates the "fight or flight" chemical adrenaline, which increases your blood pressure and heart rate and causes you to sweat profusely. Your immune system becomes less productive too.

With prolonged stress, you may suffer headaches, indigestion, nausea, rapid breathing, and a racing heart. You may also experience aches and pains. Heart attacks and strokes can result from long-term stress as well. Under stress, you may feel anxious, scared, angry, frustrated or sad. Mental health symptoms can exacerbate physical conditions.

Stress can result in changes to your behaviour. For instance, you might isolate yourself from others, have difficulty making decisions, or become irritable or aggressive towards others. Stress can also affect your sleep and mood.

It is important to realise you are suffering from stress and focus on the cause. You might need to talk to someone or take action to reduce stress levels. If you have control, take action. If you don't have control, you might need to remove yourself from a stressful environment or accept the situation. Even looking at your situation in a new light can reduce stress levels. Positive, realistic thoughts lead to positive emotions, thus reducing stress.

Since stress impacts every area of your life, it will affect your career or how you approach a career change. Therefore, it's important to have the ability to pick yourself up when life throws you a curveball.

The following tips will help you reduce stress and anxiety:
- Visualise peaceful scenery or listen to calming music. There are many guided imagery CDs and music you can buy or download.
- Practise meditation.
- Challenge negative thoughts (For example, instead of telling yourself, "I can't cope," tell yourself, "I've coped with this kind of situation before.").
- Get plenty of rest and sleep.
- Reduce your coffee or alcohol intake. These can increase symptoms of stress and affect your mood.
- Cultivate a support network of family and friends. If you are not getting support, let significant others know exactly what you need. Maybe you need validation and acknowledgment of how badly you're feeling, and that's okay.
- Join a social club or a club based on your interests, such as a book club or a chess club. Social connection is important for general well-being.

- Engage in activities that provide a sense of mastery or achievement as well as activities that give you a sense of joy and pleasure.
- Develop structure and routine to allow your body to maintain balance and harmony. Increase your activity level to enhance motivation. Ensure you repeat the same activity a few times to impact your motivational levels. The more times you repeat a behaviour, the more motivated you will be.
- Be assertive. Learn to say no, particularly to avoid burnout and stress. Know what you and your body can handle. Use "I statements" to assert your human rights. For example, "I would appreciate if you could stop making those joking remarks that are hurtful."
- Exercise regularly. Research states that thirty minutes of exercise twice a week is ideal, but do whatever you can manage to strengthen your muscles and improve your mood.
- It's important to live by your values and follow your vision and life plan—your calling. Something in life will give you purpose. If it's not your current career, you either need to change your career or find your purpose outside of your career. It's crucial to find a creative outlet that allows you to practise your passion. Even if you can't leave your job, you still have the weekends or evenings, so go for it!

I find that people experience a lot of anxiety about changing careers, starting a new career, or returning to work after a long absence. That's all part of the normal human experience, but if you don't face that anxiety, it will never go away. Instead, anxiety will be an ongoing part of your life that restricts you and makes your life smaller. Do you want to live in a restricted way and avoid certain situations or people? Do you think by avoiding anxiety, it will magically disappear? Think again!

Contribute to society in some way, however big or small, and give yourself the self-confidence you deserve. Don't remain a victim unless you truly need help to overcome your sense of safety. Some people have experienced traumatic events and need time to work through it. However, others experience anxiety that can be easily worked through with good old-fashioned will power. Having a range of coping strategies to manage stress is effective for career change and overall physical, mental, and spiritual health.

Chapter Nine:

Implement a Good Diet or Health Plan

Diet is important for holistic well-being, which affects your ability to be successful in your chosen career. All foods contain substances that hinder or help physical and mental health, so it's important to eat the right foods so you have the energy and health to pursue or manage a new career.

According to the Mental Health Foundation, certain foods contain nutrients that assist with particular mental health conditions or issues. For instance if you are under stress, you may need vitamin B6, found in whole grains such as brown rice, oats, and barley as well as bananas, mango, fish, chicken, lima beans, soy beans, and chickpeas.

Vitamin B3 changes food into glucose, which the body uses to create energy. It also reduces cholesterol and helps the brain, skin, and stomach to function. Foods with vitamin B3 include whole grains such as wheat germ, as well as broccoli, mushrooms, cabbage, peanuts, pumpkin or sunflower seeds, baked beans, bananas, kiwi fruit, and chocolate.

Magnesium produces energy in the body. It also lowers blood pressure, forms healthy bones, and helps with concentration and memory. Foods containing magnesium include spinach, avocado, broccoli, almonds, cashews, peanuts, pumpkin or sunflower seeds, long grain rice, plain yoghurt, baked beans, kiwi fruit, blackberries, strawberries, and chocolate.

The lists I've given are not exhaustive. You can find more information on the Mental Health Foundation website - https://www.mhfa.org.au for information about mental health and diet.

The Mental Health Foundation also says that people who report mental health issues tend to eat few healthy foods such as vegetables, fresh fruit, natural foods, and homemade meals. They tend to eat less healthy foods such as chips, sweets, takeaways, and processed foods.

In today's society, there is more demand for processed foods due to busy lifestyles. The result is a lower intake of fresh and healthy foods and an increase in consumption of saturated fat, sugar, alcohol, and additives. Saturated fats are found in foods such as meat and full-fat dairy and can increase cholesterol levels, heart disease, and type II diabetes.

It's important to have a diet with necessary fats, amino acids, carbohydrates, vitamins, minerals, and water. These necessary fats include unsaturated fats (such as omega 3 fats including oily fish like salmon and sardines, eggs, lean beef, chicken, walnuts, soybeans, and canola oil). The fats in these foods are healthy and may help reduce heart disease and decrease cholesterol levels. Other foods in this category include olive oil, nuts, avocados, and peanut oil.

If you're a person who enjoys eating sweets, you should be aware that the refined sugar from sweet foods is absorbed into the bloodstream quickly. This gives you loads of energy, but the energy soon wears off and you feel exhausted. On the other hand, complex carbohydrates—whole grains, fruits, and vegetables— keep you full longer than sugary foods and are absorbed into the bloodstream more slowly. Complex carbohydrates also contain thiamine (B1), a vitamin that controls mood. Further, folate and zinc in complex carbohydrates may help improve mood for people with depression.

The National Health and Medical Research Council (NHMRC) recommends the following foods for optimal health:
- At least two servings of fruit daily
- At least five servings of vegetables daily, including starch such as potatoes or sweet corn; green or brassica (cabbage family) vegetables such as broccoli, cauliflower, or cabbage; orange vegetables such as pumpkin or carrots; legumes such

as lima beans, lentils, and chickpeas; and other vegetables such as lettuce and celery.

- Nuts and seeds such as almonds, walnuts, and pumpkin seeds. These give you plenty of energy. Be sure to note the serving size.
- Wholegrains such as wholegrain breads, cereal, rice, and pasta.
- Lean red meats; however, you should not be eating more than 455 grams of red meat per week.
- Other meat and protein alternatives such as poultry, fish, eggs, and shellfish.
- At least two to two and one-half servings of dairy foods (250 grams for one serving) for protein and calcium. These include low-fat foods such as skim milk and yoghurt or medium-fat foods such as regular milk and yoghurt. Limit cheese to 20 grams daily.
- Polyunsaturated and monounsaturated fats and oils, including olive oil. You can have two servings a day (one serving is 10 grams).

Chapter Ten:

Overcome Your Barriers

A range of barriers and limitations can impact your career choice. In my work, I have helped clients overcome many barriers, including:

- A physical injury or chronic physical or mental health condition
- Mature age (some employers prefer younger employees)
- Lack of qualifications, training, or skills
- Loss of self-confidence or low self-efficacy
- Long-term unemployment
- Carer responsibilities
- Literacy and numeracy difficulties
- Lack of job search skills due to long-term unemployment or staying in one career for many years, thus being out of touch with current job search strategies.

Let's look at each of these barriers in more details. First, the Australian Government provides disability management services to people with **health conditions and helps mature age unemployed clients** attain work. Case managers can advocate with employers, arrange a work trial or work experience program, or provide a wage subsidy (funding employment for six months). If you've experienced an injury, developed a mental illness, or suffered from a chronic physical condition, you'll require support from a career counsellor who can identify your transferable skills and help you pursue alternative career options. For example, you can take a career quiz online (www.joboutlook.gov.au, then go to Career Quiz) to identify your areas of interest and abilities and take steps to achieve goals leading to that career.

It is crucial that you sell your skills to employers and convince them that you're able to fulfil the requirements of the position in spite of health conditions.

Lack of qualifications or skills require either undergoing training or seeking volunteer work in your chosen career. You may also need to study part-time while working part-time or casually in a survival job. You might seek a mentor or role model to guide you in a particular role or industry. Regular meetings to discuss experiences, advice, and how to obtain practical experience could be a part of the mentor-student relationship. Job shadowing may also be part of the process if you're interested in pursuing a new career. By watching someone in their role, you will begin to understand the work better. You might participate and assist in the role, or you might just observe.

Apprenticeships are a possibility for younger or older people who have a formal arrangement with an employer. By undertaking work training while attending a learning institution, you're able to upskill in that area of work. You obtain the necessary qualifications through formal study or certification as well as gain practical work experience.

If you have lost self-confidence or have low self-efficacy, you may benefit from having a supportive group of people around you. You may also need counselling to address negative thoughts and challenge negative beliefs. You can increase your self-confidence by doing volunteer work and participating in productive tasks that lead to mastery. Reminding yourself of your achievements and how far you've come can also increase your confidence levels and self-efficacy. Furthermore, recalling your values (what is really important to you) and striving to achieve your goals in spite of your fears can lead you to take action and start experiencing real progress. Who says you need to listen to that voice saying, "You'll only fail. You're not good enough?"

If you're experiencing long-term unemployment, you may need training in job-seeking skills including mock interviews, help with resumes, and applying for jobs. You could also benefit by participating in volunteer work or casual work so you can develop networks in the industry of your chosen career. New training can also lead to work if the training involves a practical work placement of a certain number of hours.

If you care for children or an ill or elderly family member, you may benefit from flexibility in your work hours. You may only be able to work school hours or may need respite from your local council. Carer's Victoria can provide short-term respite until you find someone else to care for your ill or elderly family member.

If you have difficulties with literacy and numeracy, you may need literacy training. If training is not available, you might benefit from a career involving your own cultural environment. For example, if you have a Chinese background, you could work in a family-owned Chinese restaurant, as you understand the language and can relate to the culture.

If you lack job seeking skills, you can benefit from a job search group and individual help with mock interviews, job applications, and resume writing.

My role with both private clients and those in vocational rehabilitation was to address barriers to employment and provide a gradual or step-by-step approach to achieving their chosen career. If your dream career is out of reach, you can start with one or more of these stepping stones:

1. Survival Job: This is a job that provides some financial security, stability, and confidence. It's not your dream job, but you're getting out, earning an income, developing skills and confidence, and meeting new people. It's far better than staying home in the depths of despair, and it is short-term. A survival job may be a temporary job while you're studying for your dream job or looking for other work.

2. Entry-level Job: This is a job focused on a different career path. You start at the bottom and work your way up towards your dream job. The level you start with depends on your experience, training, and the local job market.

3. Transition Job: This is a job in which you move from the entry-level job toward your dream job. It takes you one step further than the entry-level job. You learn the skills needed to reach your dream job. In the case of graphic design work, for example, you may accept an assistant role for a media company and then work your way up to graphic designer.

These three pathways can eventually lead to that dream job in your chosen career. You may have struggled through the steps, but you've finally reached the endpoint. You've made it! Addressing barriers to career change provides you with broader options for selecting a career from a range of fields.

Chapter Eleven:

Work/Life Balance

Work/life balance is balancing work with other aspects of your life including relationships, hobbies, leisure, and family. There are times when work gets in the way of having productive time with your family and leisure time, such as time for exercising.

The world of work has changed. People tend to work varied hours rather than regular full-time hours. For example, people do contract work, morning, afternoon or evening shifts (depending on the career), part-time work, casual work, and project work. Having resiliency and flexibility while encountering changing environments is important when balancing work with other life aspects.

Here are tips for maintaining work/life balance:

- Prioritise your tasks at work and plan to complete less important work the next day rather than staying back.
- Evaluate your work life regularly to ensure it doesn't interfere with other areas of your life. For example, coping with changes at work more effectively will greatly improve other aspects of your life.
- Remind yourself of your values to ensure changes at work continue to align with those values. If you are miserable at work, other areas of your life will most likely be impacted.
- Decide what you're prepared to sacrifice or compromise on at work so family or friends are a priority in your life.
- Seek professional help if you're stuck in a negative work/life balance.
- If self-care is an issue, you might need a hobby, or more recovery and rest. Take whatever you need.

Assessing Your Life Stage or Milestone

Your age and stage in life influence work/life balance, career growth, and career change. Each age includes stages of development, determining where you are in your life. Whether mature or young, your developmental stage affects your choices, priorities, and pace of change; some things will be right for you and some will not be. For example, you might be at an age where career is important to you to the exclusion of all else. You might not have a partner to spend time with or need to worry about caring for children. Or you might be at an age where you'd like to balance your career with your family, realising that spending time with your family is what truly matters. You don't want to miss out on your children's growth, so you'd prefer balancing your life so career isn't the most important thing to you.

It's useful to be aware of what generally happens during various life stages.

Adults Ages 22-40

Adults at this stage want to establish and maintain their careers and relationships. This is a time when mothers give birth, affecting their chosen careers. This may lead to new careers in the future, offering more flexibility and part-time arrangements after childbirth. Young adults are just starting out in their careers, and older adults may be establishing their careers or transitioning elsewhere. For instance, as one moves closer to forty, priorities may change. Initially, the young adult was career-driven, while the older adult might focus on a better work/life balance as their family and personal life become more of a priority. It becomes more important to find meaning and develop stronger connections with family and friends.

Of course, not all older adults will transition this way, as they can be as career-driven and ambitious as they were in their twenties. Personalities, lifestyle, and absent family or social connections impact work/life balance.

Adults Ages 40-65 years

Life at this stage is about managing mortgages, financial stability, empty nest syndrome, recognition of mortality, retirement, and career peaks or changes. It is also a time of physical changes and caring for grandchildren. It's a time of experiencing death and bereavement amongst loved ones. All of these age-related changes impact career priorities and potentially lead to absences at work, a reduction of work hours, or a change in career to allow for more flexibility as one seeks more work/life balance. At around age 65, one can retire.

What stage are you at right now? What recent changes have there been in your life? How are these changes impacting your career or new employer? If you've been made redundant, are you struggling to pursue new options? If you're injured, do you need to consider alternative work or retraining? Do you need career counselling or coaching assistance?

It's important to be aware of your development in order to have an understanding of what might be natural at that age. Self-awareness and reflection can help you make the right career choices or changes.

Conclusion

Throughout this book, I have discussed holistic approaches to career guidance and counselling. I focused on strengths, values, personality style, skills, attitudes, and interests. You read about career planning action, case studies, and self-care, including stress management, diet, overcoming barriers, and work/life balance.

I do hope you find the career of your dreams, whether it's your first position or a new position that suits your lifestyle changes. Good luck!

If you enjoyed this book, please review it on Amazon here:

Your Holistic Career Path - Create Career Change, Satisfaction, and Work/Life Balance - http://mybook.to/YourHolisticCareerPath

Resources

Finding the Right Direction: Career Planning Workbook (2006)
Commonwealth of Australia

Job Outlook
http://joboutlook.gov.au

Martin Seligman
https://www.authentichappiness.sas.upenn.edu/
(Register for free. Go to Questionnaires/Get Started/ Brief
Strengths Test)

Mental Health Foundation
https://www.mhfa.org.au/

Russ Harris
https://www.actmindfully.com.au/

Self - Compassion
http://self-compassion.org

St Luke's Innovative Resources (Strength and Shadow Cards)
https://innovativeresources.org/

ABOUT THE AUTHOR

Lucy Appadoo is a prolific reader and author of the Friends In Crisis Series. After a childhood spent reading and imagining escapist worlds, Lucy has put her imagination into stories. Her work as a rehabilitation counsellor, and former work as a counsellor in private practice, have led to an interest in writing inspirational stories about authentic, driven women who manage adversity with strength and heart. She writes in the genres of romantic suspense/thrillers with significant life themes and contemporary romance.

Lucy's interests include researching crime stories and news to inspire her work, watching crime thrillers and suspenseful movies, travel, exercising, reading for entertainment or knowledge, meditation, and spending time with friends and family. She also appreciates her Italian background and culture, which has inspired her to write imaginative stories about her parents' childhoods, leading to The Italian Family Series novels.

Check out Lucy's website and sign up for a FREE romantic suspense novel here: www.lucyappadooauthor.com.au

ALSO BY LUCY APPADOO

NON-FICTION

Grief & Loss
Moving Beyond Grief - How To Shift From Grief & Loss to
Joy & Peace - http://mybook.to/MovingBeyondGrief

Stress Management & Anxiety
Holistic Spiritual and Mental Health - Building Resilience and
Creativity by Conquering Anxiety and Managing Stress -
http://mybook.to/Holistichealth

Journal and Record Of Books You've Read (with Quotes)
Readers' Journal - http://mybook.to/ReadersJournal

FICTION

The Friends In Crisis Series - Romantic Suspense/Thriller
Haunted By The Past (Book 1) -
http://mybook.to/HauntedbythePast
Twisted Obsession (Book 2) -
http://mybook.to/TwistedObsession
Web Of Lies (Book 3) - http://mybook.to/EbookWebOfLies

The Hearts Series - Romantic Suspense
Rising Hearts (Book 1) - http://mybook.to/RisingHearts
Forbidden Hearts (Book 2) -
http://mybook.to/ForbiddenHearts
Kindred Hearts - (Book 3) - http://mybook.to/kindredhearts
Broken Hearts (prequel to Forbidden Hearts) -
http://mybook.to/Bhearts

Short Story Thrillers
Evening Interrupted - http://mybook.to/Eveninginterrupted
The Dreamcatcher - http://viewbook.at/Thedreamcatcher
Red Flags - http://mybook.to/Redflags
Collection of Short Story Thrillers -
http://mybook.to/collectionofthrillers

The Italian Family Series - Coming of Age Family Drama/Romance
A New Life - http://mybook.to/ANewLife
The Beauty of Tears - http://mybook.to/TheBeautyofTears
Dancing in the Rain - http://mybook.to/dancingintheRain
A Life By Design - http://mybook.to/Alifebydesign